Penguins

Kate Riggs

CREATIVE EDUCATION

seedlings

Published by Creative Education
P.O. Box 227, Mankato, Minnesota 56002
Creative Education is an imprint of
The Creative Company
www.thecreativecompany.us

Design and production by Ellen Huber
Art direction by Rita Marshall
Printed in the United States of America

Photographs by Alamy (Maximilian Weinzierl), Dreamstime
(Isselee, Christian Musat, Goinyk Volodymyr), Getty Images
(Bill Curtsinger, Darrell Gulin, Tui De Roy, Joseph Van
Os, Norbert Wu), Photo Researchers (William Ervin/Photo
Researchers, Inc.), Shutterstock (alterfalter, AlessandroZocc,
Anna Kucherova, Leksele), Veer (Corbis Photography)

Library of Congress Cataloging-in-Publication Data
Riggs, Kate.
Penguins / by Kate Riggs.
p. cm. — (Seedlings)
Includes index.
Summary: A kindergarten-level introduction to penguins,
covering their growth process, behaviors, the coasts they call
home, and such defining physical features as their flippers.
ISBN 978-1-60818-279-4
1. Penguins—Juvenile literature. I. Title.

QL696.S473R54 2012
598.47—dc23   2011044744

First Edition
9 8 7 6 5 4 3 2 1

TABLE OF CONTENTS

Hello, penguins!

Penguins are
birds that swim.
Most penguins
live in or near
Antarctica.

Penguins
have feathers.
They have
dark feathers
on their back.
They have
light feathers
on their belly.

Penguins have flippers.
They have webbed feet, too.

Penguins eat
small ocean animals.

They like fish such as sardines.

A baby penguin
is called a chick.
A chick lives with
other penguins
in a rookery.

Penguins
swim in
the ocean.
They chase
their food.

Penguins like to swim fast!

Goodbye, penguins!

Picture a Penguin

beak

flippers

webbed feet

eye

feathers

tail

Words to Know

Antarctica: a big piece of land covered with ice and snow

flippers: flat limbs (like arms) that help penguins swim

ocean: a big area of deep, salty water

rookery: a group of penguins that live together on land

webbed: having toes connected by flat skin

Read More

Shively, Julie. *Baby Penguin*.
Nashville: CandyCane Press, 2005.

Tatham, Betty. *Penguin Chick*.
New York: HarperCollins, 2002.

Web Sites

DLTK's Penguin Activities
http://www.dltk-kids.com/animals/birds-penguins.html
Make your own penguins out of paper!

Penguin Activities and Crafts
http://www.first-school.ws/theme/animals/birds/penguin.htm
Print out pictures to color. Then play a puzzle or do a craft!

Index